T0119070

Books published during this era were mostly written with masculine references and pronouns used to represent common examples of people in general, without implying that one gender was more entitled or more deserving than the other. As publisher, DeVorss Publications has worked over the years to enhance the meaning of many books by making subtle changes that allow the message to be all-encompassing for readers. These changes can be found in Wells of Abundance.

WELLS OF ABUNDANCE

The Seven Planes of Supply AND *The Law of Increase*

by

E. V. Ingraham

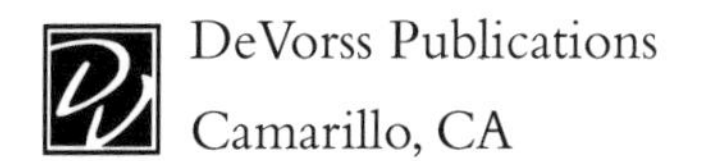
DeVorss Publications
Camarillo, CA

 This edition has been altered to neutralize many of the masculine references that were pervasive in the original edition and were accepted as standard writing style of that time.

The 2018 edition has been modified to embrace gender-neutral language and terms while preserving the author's intent and message, with the exception of direct quotes or excerpts from other sources.

PRINT ISBN: 978-087516-898-2
EBOOK ISBN: 978-087516-899-9
DeVorss & Company, Publisher
PO Box 1389
Camarillo CA 93012
www.devorss.com

Printed in The United States of America

TABLE OF CONTENTS

FIRST PLANE OF SUPPLY

The Law of Absorption

Peace be within thy walls, and prosperity within thy palaces.
PSALMS 122:7

At the root of most human difficulty lies the eternal problem of supply in some of its phases. In fact, supply must include that which supports every phase of our nature, and every difficulty involves some lack of proper support. The ancients called all imperfection a matter of "under-nourishment." To thoroughly understand the question of supply would, therefore, enable us to understand the whole problem of successful living.

There is a logic to be followed in the matter of supply. "Order is Heaven's first law" and we must learn to take first things first. If we approach supply in the order of its most vital importance, the following sequences will not be difficult. At the beginning, it should be noticed that the more necessary any element is to the sustaining of life, the more there is of it, the easier it is to contact and the more impossible it is for anyone to separate you from it or charge you anything for it. Take the following elements, and consider how relatively important they are in sustaining life; how they are increasingly available as they increase in importance:

Shelter, Clothing, Food, Water, Air, Consciousness, Hope, Aspiration—and finally, that mysterious something that is the very essence of life itself.

That which increases hope and the realization of a more abundant life would be the most essential element of supply. Faith, Prayer, Meditation, Communion with the Presence and Power of God would be the most effective means of appropriating this "inner" supply.

What would any outward attainment matter without beauty, music, fragrant odors, and the fineness of the sense of touch? Supply for this phase of our being is free and feeds the inner nature. But we must take the time to enjoy this food for our soul. The fact is that most of the supply that we work for feeds only 2% of our nature. That which feeds the other 98% is free for the effort involved in receiving. If this 98% of our nature were habitually fed, the matter of taking care of the other 2% would be simple and easy. Let us, therefore, try to consider supply in its broadest and fullest sense. Let us also be diligent in applying ourselves to every phase of supply in order that we may be most fully provided with all things needful. If we can feed some of the inner hungers first, we may find it a more simple matter to feed the remaining outer hungers.

Life is seven-fold, and supply functions on Seven Planes. In other words, there are seven degrees or ways in which supply moves. Or, we might say, there are seven ways in which we may approach the matter of supply.

The simplest form of supply is Absorption. In this field, an organism merely absorbs from its immediate surroundings all of the elements necessary to its maintenance and growth. This method of obtaining supply belongs primarily to the vegetable kingdom. From seed to fruit, a plant absorbs moisture, the elements of the earth, air, and sun. The vegetable toils not nor does it spin. It only receives.

But when human beings descend to this plane, they "vegetate" or retrograde. People belong on a plane much higher than that of the vegetable. People must learn to live upon their own plane if they are to flourish as human beings. Humans who try to live on this plane think the world owes them a living. They become leeches and parasites, expecting supply to be furnished by those who are more industrious. They are the beggars who have lost their station in life by expecting support without giving an equivalent in return. The law, "Give and it shall be given unto you" works with precision. Where there is no voluntary giving for what is received, something is taken from you.

The voluntary offering plan in the religious field has pauperized millions of people. It has not been made clear that voluntary giving is a plan for individual development. It is a way of preserving the sense of balance between people and their surroundings. Not understanding this phase of the plan, too many people have imagined that spiritual service is free and that they need only receive. Spiritual, and often physical and material, bankruptcy have been the results. Every sincere student should read Emerson's essay on "Compensation." Jesus did not teach that "salvation is free." He told the rich young man that it would require of him everything he had. "Give and it shall be given unto you" is His own statement of the law involved.

Let everyone who receives instruction or help from any spiritual avenue take due note of this law and they will doubtless find the reason for their lack of progress. If you can afford to go to picture shows, for your own sake and well-being, you can afford to sacrifice the movie if necessary to give to the one who serves you spiritually. If you have no material means to give, at least make a note of the date when service was rendered, place opposite the amount you honestly feel the service is worth. Then ask God to make it possible for you to give this amount. Pray daily for the way to be opened that you may "give as you have received." Keep it up until the way is opened, or until you have a deep conviction that God has in some way answered your prayer and made up to the individual or organization the equivalent of the spiritual service you have received.

The foregoing is not suggested with the idea of increasing the income of spiritual workers but to help the student attain a basis of more certain spiritual as well as material progress. "With what measure you mete, it shall be measured to you again." Nothing is of value to you except on the basis of value placed by yourself. It cannot truly be yours until you have given value in return for value received. Begin giving blessings, words of gratitude, prayers of abundance, gifts prepared by your own hands, or any other thing of value that occurs to you. Give to those who serve you in any way and in every way that you can devise. Then see if the blessings you have been seeking are not released to you.

You are a part of the entire Universe. You are created in the Image and Likeness of God, who is All. Therefore, every Law of Supply applies to you in some way. The Law of Absorption, or receiving, does enter into the process of your supply. However, you are primarily a spiritual being and you receive upon a spiritual plane, first, at least. Learn to receive the very essence of all things that surround you. Absorb the very presence of life, love, wisdom, power, and substance, just as you might absorb the light of the sun or the warmth of the air. Wherever you go, absorb everything that is pleasing to your soul—beauty, music, the odor of flowers. Learn to drink in everything around you that you can enjoy and appreciate.

This is all vital and essential supply. All of it feeds your inner nature. When inwardly fed, the outer supply will become simple.

By prayer, breathe in the greatness, the grandeur, the nearness of God. By meditation, receive the wisdom, the love, and the power of God. By communion, unify your nature with the essence of life, health, strength, and wealth of God. All the Universe is your storehouse from which to receive. The world is your field of radiation or expression.

MEDITATION

"Because a created Universe exists, that which produced it must have been operative prior to and during its appearance. That same force must be operative in order that creation be sustained. If this were not true, creation would vanish.

"I am not a product of the world but of the same operative principle that produced the world. Therefore, that force which sustains the Universe, sustains me. I am sustained, supported, and supplied by a self-operative process that sustains and supports the entire Universal system.

"God, who is the sum total of all the visible and invisible Universe ('I am that I am' and beside me there is no other) is both the Creator and the Created. I am, then, part of God and actually live, move, and have my being in Him. My Creator and Sustainer is in me, through me, and around me. God is the Life of my life, the Mind of my mind, and the Substance of my flesh. God is my immediate supply, the complete support of my entire being.

"My supply is at hand. It fills me, surrounds me, and is poured out upon me from everywhere. Supply flows to me wherever I am and in whatever I do. My supply is constant and exhaustless and I am richly endowed with all things in Heaven and Earth. I receive my invisible and visible supply constantly and I am increasingly rich within and without."

SECOND PLANE OF SUPPLY

The Law of Force

Charge them that are rich in this world, that they be not high-minded, nor trust (hope) in uncertain riches, but in the living God, who giveth us richly all things to enjoy.

TIMOTHY 6:17

Before taking up the study of this Second Plane of Supply, you should first make certain that you have sufficiently practiced the preceding one. All future progress in the matter of supply will be strengthened if you are grounded in the first steps. Faithfulness in first things is the secret of progress in any direction. Outer supply is often delayed because fundamental requirements have not been met. When the inner nature is fully supplied, the matter of outer supply will be easily taken care of.

Each degree of supply is only the increased momentum, or expansion, arising from a simple starting point. All that we think, say, or do regarding anything began with a simple idea. It is futile to hope for full knowledge or power in any direction except through a logical procedure from start to finish in the process.

Supply begins with the simple idea of receiving as outlined in our previous lesson. Receiving awakens increased desire and capacity and we accordingly begin to make greater demands. An individual is more than a sponge; therefore, the mere act of receiving does not meet the requirements of their more complex nature.

Moving on in the scale of supply, we find the next law to be a matter of force. This Second Plane of Supply, materially considered, belongs to the carnivorous animals. These animals get their supply by forcefully taking it from others. In most cases, they prey upon the lesser beasts. When this Law of Supply is employed, one descends to the animal plane and becomes the thief, the robber, the grafter, the racketeer, the extortionist, and the usurer. By force, cunning, deception, or advantage, they prey upon those who have. That person is not intelligent enough to use their skill and talents to produce for themselves. They devote all their energy to getting what others have produced. Such people are vultures and beasts of prey in human guise.

Descending to a plane beneath the human status exacts its terrific toll, for the law of compensation is exact. Such humans lose their peace of mind, their sense of security, their liberty, and often life itself. They lose their self-respect and the respect of those about them. One can maintain his/her standing in the world as a respected person only if one lives as a respectable person. We are co-creators with the Source, and to find the fullness of life, we must become a producer and not live by what others produce.

Being a replica of the Universe (the image and likeness of God) has something of every plane within each person. The application of the various laws must be according to this high estate. We are spiritual beings and the application of the Law of Force is on a spiritual, not a physical, plane. It may be a new idea to you that force is a Law of Supply on the spiritual plane. Nevertheless, it is so. "The Kingdom of Heaven suffereth violence and the violent take it by force."—Matt. II:12. Force here has no semblance to the forceful measures characteristic of the material or animal world.

Human beings too easily surrender to the apparent. A little positive assertion is often all that is necessary to turn the tide of events. Sometimes a more enduring persistence is necessary. But the tide must be turned if we are to rise into the realm of creative intelligence where we belong.

Jacob wrestled with the angel all night before he received the blessing. A little wrestling with facts will inevitably break the struggle with appearances. And the chances are that if we do not exert the necessary force in wrestling with facts, we will have plenty of opportunity to struggle with the apparent.

Ordinarily, breathing is a process of simply absorbing or inhaling the air. But if you have ever had the "wind knocked out of you," that simple process of absorbing air was not sufficient to meet the situation. You had, in this instance, to fight for the air. Some force had to be exerted. Perhaps, at times, you have had to fight for your reason in very much the same way. At times, you have faced a difficult rule, or complex saying. The ordinary process by which the mind absorbs—easily comprehends—does not seem to suffice. A definite assertion of the mind, a forceful effort to drive the mind until it penetrates through to the meaning seems necessary.

The foregoing may serve to somewhat illustrate that manner of force as applied to our supply. When you get the "financial wind knocked out of you," so to speak, it may be necessary to forcefully drive the mind in the direction of your Source. "God is our supply" is a recognized fact, but to clearly remember and realize this fact in the face, of outer lack is where the test comes in. At such times a "wrestling" with the spiritual fact seems essential. If no positive effort is put forth in this direction, you are likely to curl up in the cruel clutches of poverty and defeat. "Watch ye, stand fast in the faith, quit you like men, be strong" advised Paul in the way of human progress.

Exercising force in the matter of supply is not exercising the will or driving the flesh to get outer results. It is exerting the will to the point of complete reliance upon God as not only the Source but the Supply itself. Faith is a much greater force than the Will. Will is only efficient when used to awaken or conform to faith. Faith is real wealth, for it is a force that produces. Dare to trust, dare to rely, dare to have faith that God is your instant and manifest supply even when you cannot see it. Faith sees into realms where the eye of the mind and the eyes of the flesh cannot see. "If ye have faith and doubt not, nothing shall be impossible to you." If this statement of the Christ be true, as it undoubtedly is, faith is an irresistible and an all-achieving force. By it, people force themselves out into the facts of life, and these facts are omnipotent.

Living in faith, one comes to the point of Knowing. "Knowledge is power," we have so often been reminded. Here again, we have another transcendent force. It keeps one calm in calamity and victorious in seeming defeat. The outcome is seen and known, therefore, the incidents intervening are of little consequence. "Knowing" acts like magnetic force in a bar of steel. Its power of attraction is irresistible. It pulls into being that to which it is attached. If you are knowingly convinced of poverty, there is no human power that can prevent poverty from springing into manifestation all around you. If you have a knowing realization that the abundance of God is yours, all the forces of Heaven and Earth contrive with you until abundance is manifest in everything that concerns you.

Learn to reach out into the Universe. Absorb all that it naturally radiates toward you. Once the sense of its abundance awakens in you, a great hunger for more will also awaken. Then you will wrestle with the wealth that is there for you until it is visibly manifest in your mind, body, and affairs. The wealth of the Universe is yours. Take it! The timid seldom arrive at great fulfillment. The bold, like Paul who dared, and Christ who fearlessly faced reality, know the thrill and realization of the abundance of God!

MEDITATION

"I arise and go unto God's house where there is enough to spare. I refuse to be drawn into the entangling illusion of appearances. I dare to risk my all to the sustaining Power who created me. If I am a created being, the Power that created me must be the Source of all that I have and am. Since God is the Source, it must be the Life, the Substance, and sustaining Power of my whole being. My Supply, then, is immediately at hand and instantly available to me.

"I wrestle with the unalterable fact that 'God is my Supply' until I see it, feel it, and know it. Nothing matters to me now but the comprehension, the knowing of this fact. I apply myself to it day by day. I pursue it in all that I say, think, and do. Awake or asleep, my whole being constantly and intently pursues the truth until I possess it in the secret depths of my own soul.

"When I sufficiently know this fact in my own soul, then I shall equally know its manifestation in my outer affairs.

"God is my supply. The Spirit and Substance of Abundance fills me and surrounds me. It feeds my flesh, revives my mind, restores my soul. It fires me with renewed power and creative ability and I am aroused in the might and power of the inner man. Wealth of Heaven and Earth is mine and I am rich in the priceless knowledge that 'all that God hath is mine.' "

THIRD PLANE OF SUPPLY

The Law of Work

The blessing of the Lord maketh rich and addeth no sorrow thereto.

PROVERBS 10:22

The Third Plane of Supply is where it is earned by work. This is where an individual, who considers themselves a mere human being, should logically expect their supply. But to work only for what you can get is but little better than the thief. You have not yet caught up with the law of compensation but it is still at work in you. Until you reach the place where there is a free giving for what you are receiving, you are never on a secure footing. Your salary is or should be a just balance for the service you give. To advance, you must get ahead of the law and begin to give more than you receive. Sooner or later, you will see the law of balance at work. Your increased supply will inevitably come. Profit and service in righteous balance is what makes this Plane pleasingly effective.

"One profits most who serves best" is not a mere axiom, but it is a living truth. Voluntary giving of the best you are capable of giving takes the place of exacted toll. Then the returns begin to voluntarily increase.

Following this procedure, it finally dawns on you that a sort of mysterious change has taken place. At first, you were always trying to get something. Now the very thing you were trying to get is seeking you. This new thing also has a way of compounding itself. Not only do you receive more return for your work, but new opportunities for work with still greater returns present themselves. This is one of the most joyous experiences in the path of life. There comes the sense that you are not only making real progress but that you are in harmony with the Law of Life.

When working, men and women realize that work is for the purpose of expressing and developing skill, there will be no drudgery in their labors. When industries operate primarily as schools of skill, problems between capital and labor will vanish. The returns for both will increase and satisfaction will prevail. Each pursuing a motive in which they both agree and profit, they will both attain perfect results. When the motive of both is to get, there can be nothing but turmoil, strife, and ultimate war.

When one realizes the entire motive of work is the development and expression of skill—a means of growth and advancement—then the individual has reached the turning point in the matter of supply. Work, then, loses its strenuousness and becomes a fascinating pursuit. You will also discover that the same degree of joy and eagerness in this motive is returned in the good that comes back to you. The law gives back in exact ratio and kind, that which you express in giving. Once this process is clearly experienced, one becomes as fascinated with their work as in the most intriguing game.

"Wealth gotten by vanity shall diminish; but he who gathereth by labor shall increase." One may find courage in the possibilities of securing work if they will contemplate a statement of Gladys M. Relyea in *Collier's* for April 30, 1938, that "according to occupational experts, there are 25,000 ways to make a living in the United States." This information should be interesting enough to instigate everyone looking for opportunities for service instead of explaining how and why there is nothing to do.

Once abundance is attained, there is a greater need of inward ability than before, because both yourself and your money must be sustained. "The sleep of a laboring man is sweet whether he eat little or much; but the abundance of the rich will not suffer him to sleep."—Eccl. 5 :12. Unless strong character is built in our accumulation of outer wealth, we only get into greater unrest than before.

Physical work is only a means of outward expression. It builds muscle but not character. It is the working of the mind behind the muscle that builds skill. The attitude in work makes character. Motives govern the whole nature of the outer man. Ability is fed from inner sources of supply and only when we are inwardly fed, can we expect the outer nature to be well.

Mental and spiritual work are the first tasks of the individual who would express the greatest achieving power in the world. A proper conditioning of the soul is fundamentally important in all undertakings. Outer work can be no more effective than the motives that prompt the performance of tasks, just as the performance of an engine is no better than the fuel used in it. The kind of inner work that builds up the highest and most vital motives should be the first consideration. We so often make the mistake of tackling the outer aspect of a problem before we have mastered its inner aspect. In supply, we should first work to master the sense of lack by building an inner sense of wealth. This is done by prayer, meditation, and the intelligent use of affirmation.

Prayer is not a mere petition addressed to God in the hope that we will be given money, or even bread. Of course, it is all right to pray for both money and bread. But it is more important to pray that the spirit of abundance fill your heart and mind. One should pray for the consciousness that "all that my Source hath is mine." Pray that the bounty of the Universe, the wealth of Heaven and Earth so fill you that you feel the riches of your true estate as an actual inner possession. Pray that you be so filled with the abundance of God that even outer poverty could not impress you or affect you in the least.

Meditation is dwelling upon and quietly analyzing the basic facts of life. Meditation is a sort of inward prayer, that process of mind whereby you accept and digest the facts aroused in prayer. Here, you think deeply regarding the fact that the activity of God has created you out of its own substance; that this activity must involve the complete nature of God; that this complete nature of God moves within you now; and that because of this activity, you are constantly sustained spiritually, strengthened physically, and illumined mentally. The activity of God upon you and through you is a vital stream of supply that provides the most essential elements of life. This sense of the Universal and inward flow of supply must sooner or later loosen every element of outward supply and move visible abundance to you. "Straws show which way the wind blows" and driftwood follows the current of the stream. So does your outer supply flow on the current of inward supply.

Affirmation, another phase of spiritual work, is a definite laying hold of an attitude of accepting and appropriating supply that has been uncovered and set into operation by prayer and meditation. Affirmation does not take the place of prayer and meditation, but it does supplement and coordinate them with the outer world. Give yourself daily to your spiritual work in the matter of supply. Keep the mind first interested in the spiritual sense of supply. Only let the mind turn to include outer supply when the inner realization is strong throughout your entire nature.

MEDITATION

"Almighty God, Source of all creation, flood me with thy light and life. Pour out your whole spirit and substance upon me and supply me richly with all the fullness of your bounty. Let thy exhaustless wealth enrich my spirit, endow my soul, and fill my mind with the riches of the Kingdom.

"In gratitude, I receive the blessing of the Holy Spirit. In the depths of my being I meditate and ponder the great wealth that I daily and hourly receive from thy rich storehouse. Thy substance fills my whole being and I am richly blessed with every good and perfect gift coming from the Source of Light. 'All the wealth of the Universe is mine.' The riches of Heaven and Earth flow to me and I am made rich within and without."

FOURTH PLANE OF SUPPLY

The Law of Attraction

This book of the law shall not depart out of thy mouth; but thou shalt meditate therein day and night, that thou mayest observe to do according to all that is written therein: for then thou shalt make thy way prosperous, and then thou shalt have good success.

JOSHUA 1:8

By this time in our study and practice, we begin to realize that supply is not so much a matter of material form as of spiritual forces. Furthermore, as we avail ourselves of the ever-accessible spiritual forces, it is much easier to gain the material forms. This experience may be continued indefinitely, and the more this order of supply is followed, the more readily the outer supply comes. The ultimate, of course, is the discovery of the secret of instant fulfillment. This is the fascinating goal ahead of the faithful.

When one really breaks through into the realization of the power of this procedure, a great sense of freedom comes. It is like passing from a stuffy room into the freedom of the great out-of-doors. Every weight of lack and oppression of poverty falls off and you clearly sense the presence of Divine Wealth. Abundance fills and vitalizes the very air you breathe. Instead of forebodings of lack, you are filled with the promise of abundance. When the might and power of inner strength is supplied, the whole aspect of life changes.

In this stage of progress in developing inner supply, you find that the things you formerly pursued are now seeking you. A sort of inner magnetic force seems to attract jobs, opportunities, money. This Law of Attraction is the Fourth Plane of Supply. At this point, to strengthen your knowledge of the process involved, we suggest that you buy a small horseshoe magnet, such as boys play with. Spend some time each day watching needles, pins, and metal objects jump to it until it dawns upon you that a radiant, inner force always has power to attract its own kind from the world of form.

Now consider your own being in place of the magnet and your own deep feelings in place of the magnetic force. Here you have the key by which all manner of things are attracted to you. A feeling and conviction of poverty attracts poverty conditions in the world of form. A feeling and conviction of abundance attracts outer abundance.

Go on from here, and realize that all of your procedure up to and including this point is only for the purpose of building up the forces of your inner nature until they are so strong that outer evidences of supply begin to move toward you. Do not spend your time merely hoping and expecting everything to come to you. Be equally willing and ready to go to them. But above all, be continually active in building and maintaining the realization that the abundance of the Universe is yours, that it flows to you from every source, and that the Law of Attraction opens wide every channel of supply. Meditate much along this line of thought: "I Am Filled with the Wisdom, Love, Power, and Substance of God, and as an Irresistible Magnet, I Draw to Me All That Is Needful for My Most Complete Expression in Life."

In following this practice, do not keep one eye open to see if things are coming your way. This dividing your attention only delays the process. Keep everlastingly at work in filling yourself with the ever-present abundance of God—His Wisdom, Love, Power, and Substance. You will ultimately notice the change in the attitude of everything and everybody toward you. This course of action has been known to build a successful business and eventually, to sell it at a profit. It will accomplish remarkable results for anyone who will faithfully follow it.

In taking up this method of spiritual work, one does not cease to work outwardly. In fact, one does more outward work and that work is the more effective. It is also joyous work. But the motive is completely reversed. You work always to increase your realization of spiritual power and abundance, KNOWING that all the Universe is working with you, guiding your mind, feeding and supplementing your ability and sustaining your flesh. You become acutely aware that the "Spirit of God works through you to will and to do that which ought to be done by you." What you thus build into your character attracts to you from the world that which exactly conforms to your newly awakened realization.

When we begin to see that the foregoing is an accurate explanation of why certain things come to us, we will also understand what we have previously considered rank injustice. We have so often asked why certain people, apparently good, faithful, and sincere workers, are always getting the "tough breaks." You see, it is not what we seem to do or be in the outer that counts most. "Man looketh on the outward appearance, but God looketh upon the heart." What goes on inside of our consciousness is what determines the status of our outer life. "To him that hath shall be given" and it is given in kind and degree according to what you have. What you have is what you are most conscious of in your mind and feeling nature. That is what determines your power of attraction.

The purpose of life must take into first consideration the perfecting of our inner self—not the accumulation of money and possessions. Only as someone grows in wisdom and power can they expect their outer world to grow. The outer must and always will be a product of the inner. One can, therefore, see that the important thing in supply is to build up the consciousness and realization of abundance. Money does not build the consciousness of abundance and security. True, it helps if we are proceeding correctly. But the inner realization of God's Infinite Abundance will produce a sense of security and money as well.

Your world changes as inevitably and under the same law as the expression on your face changes. It is not the smile that makes a joyous heart, but a joyous heart that produces the smile. This same law applies to the condition of your body generally, to your clothes, your home, your business, and your finances as well. "With what measure you mete, it shall be measured to you again." What you radiate determines what your manifest world will be.

If you have had any difficulty in demonstrating supply or business, try forgetting the outer manifestations for a time and give yourself to the meditations at the close of this lesson. Devote yourself to them with the single purpose of building a strong realization of the facts indicated. Remember, it is a matter of building up your spirit, of increasing the forces of abundance within yourself. Potential wealth exists as your storehouse of inner powers and capacities. The realization of eternal facts and the consciousness that all of the wealth of the Universe is yours comprise your limitless supply. And, "he that hath the spirit hath the sign also." Fill your heart, soul, and mind with the treasures of Heaven, then you will have an abundance of the world's wealth. It will come to you as truly as iron filings are attracted to a magnet.

MEDITATION

"All the creative power and intelligence of God fills and surrounds my entire being. This power has created me; out of its substance, my body and my world have been formed. The Presence of God with me and in me sustains, feeds, and nourishes me in soul, in mind, and in flesh. Only the Spirit that created me can sustain me. Therefore, I feast upon the Spirit of God's abundance that is now and eternally poured out upon me from the four corners of the Universe. I receive it, accept it, and build it into my consciousness and character. It is my light, my life, and my substance.

"I am filled with the wisdom, love, power, and substance of God. They feed and nourish my whole being from within. Refreshed in the knowledge and power of God, I am supplied with the original essentials of life. Being filled with the Spirit and radiant in the consciousness of God's rich abundance, I am an irresistible magnet that draws to me all material things needful to my completeness and perfection."

FIFTH PLANE OF SUPPLY

Supply as an Inheritance

The Lord knoweth the days of the upright;
and their inheritance shall be forever.
PSALMS 37:18

It is a self-evident fact that the more frequently you associate with anything, the more you feel a part of it and the more its operations vitally affect you.

Spiritual practice is no exception to this rule. The faithful application of spiritual law brings a consciousness that you are not a product of, nor a part of, a material world. Everything seems to move out and become a part of the larger system. As the poet has said:

"Nothing in this world is single;
All things by a law Divine,
With one another's being mingle."

The world did not produce itself and it did not produce the things that live upon it. The things that appear upon the earth are but further expressions of the same system that produced it in the first place. Should the Universal system break down, then every part of the system would break down. It can then be seen that even a single blade of grass is supported by the Universal system. This entire system is, of course, God who is Creator, Ruler, and Sustainer of the system. You, a part of this creation, are also a product of the same Infinite system. You are a more complete expression, the very "image and likeness of God" and "a little lower than the angels." You are, therefore, the highest in line of succession; the highest in material form. You are necessarily sustained from the same Source.

The Law of Nature causes a plant to grow, provides all of its requirements, and sustains the plant as it is growing. There is no support for any element aside from the Principle that produced it. But here is the point to be clearly fixed in the mind if this step in supply is to be fully realized: the world, the plant, the animal, and you had nothing whatever to do with creation. At a certain point in your growth, you awakened to the fact that you were a conscious being. That being the case, the Universe—God—is solely responsible for your being here. The Universe, therefore, owes you a living, is glad to give it to you and furthermore, it is your natural heritage. Please note this statement again: "The Universe owes you a living"—not the world! As the child of God, you naturally inherit all the supply and support that is necessary for you to continue to express that which has progressed to this point. In the Lord's prayer, Christ taught us to pray "Give us this day our daily bread." He was calling your attention to your inheritance. He did not tell you to ask for what belonged to another. He told you distinctly to ask for something that is already yours. Truly, the Universe owes you a living. Not only that, but it is willing and eager to give it to you. It is God's "pleasure to give you the Kingdom." Nothing but the Universal system can sustain you, for the Creator is both the life and substance of the created. We cannot live by bread alone. Quite truly we cannot, for bread does not feed our mind, spirit, or life.

You should dwell much upon the fact that you are more dependent upon invisible forces than forms for your support. Think often how much more your nature depends upon air than water, and so on. What keeps your mind going, what feeds your hopes and ideals? What keeps your life going on and on? It is best for your own progress that you trace these answers through for yourself.

Someday, if you will be faithful to this practice, the whole matter of supply will clear up.

Then go on with the idea that air is something you inherit in the very process of living. It is yours by right, and no one can rob you of it nor can they charge you for it. From here on to the highest forces of the Universe, you inherit all things. They are yours by Divine right. All that the Source has is yours. Yours now, not something you come into possession of at a later date. It is all yours, an inheritance now! "To as many as receive my Spirit, to them is given power to become the Children of God."

The prodigal son understood this matter of inheritance and he said to his father: "Give me that portion of thy goods that falleth to me." He understood that certain things were naturally his. He asked for his own and received it. Up to this point, he was entirely within his right. His mistake was in separating himself and his inheritance from his father, spending it in riotous living. Up to the point of his separation, he was obeying Christ's instruction "Give me this day my daily bread." This is not only a request for your own supply, your inherited support from the System, but it is claiming it for today. Now is the only time you can accept supply.

Claiming, accepting, receiving, and building this Universal supply into your character is a most vital and satisfying procedure. By it, you get back into harmony with basic facts, and the sense of wealth and security become living realities to you. Here outer supply seems eagerly seeking you. The magnet here works stronger than ever. You realize as a practical reality the statement made earlier in these lessons that "outer supply rides on the current of your inner supply."

This practice leads to an actual inrush of your supply. Abundance begins to crowd in upon your mind and feeling. You know the negative experience of this stage of realization when trouble or lack crowd in. This stage of your progress is just the reverse aspect of the same law. The sword of the Spirit has two edges and cuts both ways. Before, nothing in the whole kingdom of life seemed to be yours. Now, everything in Heaven and Earth seems to be yours. "My supply, as my inheritance, has arrived. It is mine! It is my birthright." Knowing your own is a sort of coming of age spiritually.

The absolute knowing that a thing is yours is an irresistible force. "That which I know is mine must come to me by the very law of my being." Did you ever see in a store window some garment that exactly suited you? In that moment of supreme oneness with the garment, did you brand it by saying, "That is mine"? Then, did you later see it in the same store, back in the department from whence it came, and still later find it on the bargain counter? Did you wonder why no one ever bought it? Your stamp of ownership was indelibly impressed upon it, and no one could buy it. It could not suit anyone else, for your consciousness was so completely incarnate in it. But to merely claim things does not bring them to you, even though you may take them out of circulation for others. If you knew your Divine supply as firmly, as feelingly, as spontaneously, you would have enough to procure anything in the outer that you needed. Therefore, assume the attitude of an inheritor, a feeling that you inherit the abundance of God. Keep it up until the radiant sense of "mine" comes over you. Here you will enter into a new and wonderful world where you belong. You will be back where there is enough and to spare.

You will still work. But your work will not be labor for reward. It will be the joyous expression of such inward wealth that you must work to express the great joy and abundance of life. You work in order that others may be enriched by your efforts.

MEDITATION

"Being a product of the creative Law of the Universe, I inherit all of the Life, Intelligence, and Substance of Infinite Space (God). God has created me as a vehicle through which I express in my life. As God has given me my being, I am an expression of the Life, Intelligence, and Substance of Infinite Space so that the pleasure may be complete and continuous. I constantly inherit all things, for it is the will and pleasure of God to give and express through me.

"All that the Universal Source hath is mine! Give me this day my daily bread! Give me now, the fullness of supply that is rightfully mine! Let my rightful Inheritance flow from Heaven and Earth as it is ordained from the beginning.

"The Power, the Life, the Intelligence, and the Substance of God are forever mine. They are mine by the law of birth. They are mine now and I receive them with gratitude. I claim my Inheritance of Wisdom also that I may use my vast Inheritance to the Honor and Glory of My Source. I accept and receive my Inheritance of all good that the 'Glory of God' may be made manifest through me."

SIXTH PLANE OF SUPPLY

Supply and the Creative Process

For the seed shall be prosperous, the vine shall give her fruit, and the ground shall give her increase, and the heavens shall give their dew; and I will cause the remnant of this people to possess all these things.

ZECHARIAH 8:12

How fascinating this whole matter of supply becomes as its various phases unfold. Like everything else, it unfolds only to those who study it. We discover only what we search for. This explains why so many of us have not found and manifested abundance. We really have not searched for it. The discovery of supply is not only interesting because the supply itself is desirable; but the progressive unfoldment of the idea is fascinating in itself. It is like finding the solution to a puzzle or discovering the secret of some very complex situation. Once this point of fascination has been reached, the rest of our progress will be easier.

The Sixth Plane of Supply brings a new and more fascinating discovery. As we search out the mystery of supply, we find that something vastly more important is involved in the process. It is something that sets aside all the struggle and uncertainty in our pursuit of the needful things in life.

Wherever there is an inheritance, there must be a source from which it originated. Furthermore, there must have been a willingness and an activity that the inheritance pass from the source to the inheritor. A gift implies a giver and the act of giving. There is an impelling force and actual movement that urges the gift or inheritance upon you. This, after all, is the real principle of nature. Seemingly, vegetation absorbs its supply from the sun, air, and earth. But in reality, its supply is forced upon it. It is the activity of its inheritance that supplies it with life, action, and form and is that which causes growth. Its supply is, therefore, an active process already providing needful elements before it starts to grow and continuing during its entire process of development. If this were not true, it is very evident that there would be no vegetation in the first place. "Consider the lilies of the field, how they grow" was not a mere beautiful phrase but also contains practical knowledge for those who would stop to "consider." Here is an illustration to prove that your supply is always in operation, moving upon you from every direction, offering you the wealth of Heaven and Earth. But it seems, we are not in accord with the natural process of life.

"It is God's good pleasure to give you the Kingdom." "The blessing of the Lord maketh rich and addeth no sorrow thereto." It is God who "giveth power to get wealth." How such statements take on new meaning when seen in this light. How heartening even to consider that every moment of your life your good is seeking you out; that all things needful for your progress are moving toward you. But to awaken to the realization of this fact is to arise to the state of absolute certainty in the entire matter of supply.

Certainly all creation proceeded from an active process, or there could not have been any creation. As certainly, that process must continue, or creation would disappear. If the active process contained that which produced form, it also contains all the necessary elements to sustain that form. God must be more than the life of all creation; God is the actual substance as well. Supply is, therefore, an active movement of all elements necessary to sustain and maintain your entire being. All the abundance of Heaven and Earth is always moving toward you. The supply itself has really produced you, and you belong to and in it, in a more vital sense than it belongs to you. It is not so much that you inherit it—though this is true—but in a truer sense, it has projected you; you are its expression. The law has forced itself out through you and is continually trying to force itself out more and more through you. This is where the whole idea of our Divine lineage comes in and on this bond rests the whole Law of Inheritance.

It was Emerson who wrote:

"Hast not thy share?
Lo, it rushes thee to meet.
All that nature made thine own,
Floating in air or pent in stone,
Shall rive the hills and swim the sea
And, like thy shadow, follow thee."

Perhaps you can better understand the terrific urge for your supply to express in you if you think for a moment how all living forces move toward expression. Notice all the eagerness that impels you to tell everything you know, or to express what you feel, or produce what you idealize. The desire for full expression seizes your whole nature whenever creative ideals fill you. The singer longs to sing, the dancer to dance, the artist to paint. The whole process of life in Heaven and Earth is a dynamic and irrepressible movement toward manifestation. It is upon the tide of such a force that all of your supply moves toward you. The faithful practice of the preceding steps should, here now, have brought you into perfect accord with this process. If so, your supply should spring forth speedily and abundantly.

But again, remember that "outer supply moves on the tide of the inner." Do not be drawn away from the realization of this self-acting, eager force that moves to supply you with every good and perfect gift. Too much concern about results will insulate you from its full and free expression through you. To live in absolute assurance that the results are inevitable is to keep the circuit through you flowing at full force.

Supply is really the "follow-up" or continued action of the process that created you. That being true, your full supply is guaranteed as long as the creative process is operative. You need not fear that this supply will pass in your lifetime, for the things of God are the "same yesterday, today, and forever."

Here is another vital fact that appears in considering supply at this point. Since it moves eternally, all that you have not used is cumulative. It is stored up for you, just as water has piled up behind a dam. That is the cause of the pressure you feel. You think the pressure is the weight or oppression of lack, but it is not. It is the pressure of your Universal bank account, the unused resource of your nature that is crowding itself upon you. Did you ever notice how prolific the fruit crop is when late frosts or other causes have kept the trees from bearing one or more years? Did you ever observe how much better one's health often is after a "sick spell"? Life moves on and unless we keep up with it, we feel its pressure. Someday, you must express the abundance of Spirit. It is the order of life. All that you have lacked is stored up back of your nature. It is a priceless Universal bank account waiting for you to adjust yourself to its tendency, that it may flood you with blessings until you shall be unable to contain them all.

The great secret in swift results either in healing or supply is in the knowledge that Omnipotence moves upon you to heal, to bless, and to prosper you. Study this law, watch for its action wherever you go, consider it until at last you grasp it. Then the abundance of Heaven and Earth is yours.

"Neither come I of myself, but God hath sent me."—John 8:42. The same force that sent all and sustained all. It also "healed them everyone." The same Power that sent you will sustain and heal you, if you receive!

MEDITATION

"The same Power that produced Heaven and Earth must necessarily sustain them. The Power that created must be the Life and Substance of the created. That Power moved to create and must now move to sustain. These facts must stand as the eternal law of being.

" Therefore, 'My supply of all good is at hand. The Wealth of Heaven and Earth move toward me on the current of Infinite creative Power. The tide of God's creative Power, the Spirit of God that moved to create, still moves. It moves to sustain me and all creation. It moves with pleasure to express and to fulfill itself in me here and now. With eagerness, it floods my whole being, pressing itself out into complete expression through my mind and flesh and into my affairs.'

"I inherit the Wealth of the Universe and it eagerly and actively seeks me out, pouring its great Wealth upon me. The Riches of the Kingdom flood my whole being.

"I am richly and abundantly supplied within and without from the eager storehouse of the Universe, a supply that is more eager to manifest Wealth through me than I am eager to receive it. I open my whole being wide that the eager abundance of God may enrich me and all of my world."

SEVENTH PLANE OF SUPPLY

Supply in the Absolute

For the earth shall be filled with the knowledge of the glory of the Lord, as the waters cover the sea.

HABAKKUK 2:14

It may be a bit difficult for those unaccustomed to considering abstract things to grasp supply in its absolute sense. This is a realization that one is more likely to grow into than to grasp off-hand. But to those who can grasp it, it is the direct approach to both supply and health. It all centers around the fact that cause and effect are one, that they are always synonymous and therefore, simultaneous. "If it is true of God, it must be true in manifestation" is its logic. But the mind schooled to appearances does not readily grasp this. Such a mind trying to apply this logic creates a conflict in one's nature and confusion and vague uncertainty results.

One who does not readily grasp the idea of this plane had better approach it by the easy stages of the preceding lessons. But those who can at least sense its truth will find swift progress in following this highest fact; it can hardly be called law, for it is not a movement by which results are realized but rather self-evident and self-expressed facts.

The process by which we arrive at this state might be likened to a very wealthy man falling asleep and dreaming he was very poor. In the dream, he may have all the experiences and feelings of poverty, but it would only be a dream. Finally, he awakens and his wealth is there. The only attainment involved is to "wake up." A man once explained his escape from danger in the same way. He dreamed a lion sprang upon him. He was so frightened, he awoke and, of course, he awakened to safety because there was no lion there.

All sense of lack and disease has always been classed as "illusion" by those who have attained illumination—those who have awakened. They tell us that we are held in "earth sleep" but that when we awake, we shall "see the Truth as it is." It is the exact difference between ignorance and knowledge.

An acceptable and understandable basis of reason to which the absolute approach may be compared is in the simple fact that 1 plus 1 equals 2. Now if I have no figures to express this fact, the fact still remains does it not? If I say it equals nothing, or if I say it equals three, you still hold to the fact that 1 plus 1 equals 2, do you not? Well, in this you are using the same type of reasoning that is employed in the absolute approach to supply. If God is, then supply is. If God is manifest, then your supply is manifest, but you have to wake up to the fact. In Revelations 2:9, we read, "I know thy works, and tribulations, and poverty (but thou art rich)." This is a proclamation of fact, regardless of appearances to the contrary. In like manner, we must school ourselves to facts until we awaken and see the truth thereof. When we see and know the truth, we are free of the illusion.

The individual attains to the Seventh Plane of Supply—Supply in the Absolute—only when they have expanded their consciousness to comprehend the Universality of all things visible and invisible and have entirely lost the sense of separateness. There is no longer thee and me, God and us; there is only God. The highest consciousness of supply comes when you have so completely lost yourself in the Infinite that you no longer think or speak as being in any sense apart from God. As Longfellow wrote:

" . . . we no longer entertain our
Own imperfect thoughts and vain opinions;
But God alone speaks in us and we wait
In singleness of heart that we may know
His will and in the silence of our spirits
That we may do His will and do that only."

A sponge immersed in water becomes completely saturated with it. It returns to the state of complete oneness with the environment in which it grew. So as we, returning to our Source, abiding in it, reach the point of complete saturation. We are one in and with our Source: "I and God are one." Here you are in God's house and "all thine is mine and all mine is thine." To comprehend this basic and unalterable fact is to be absolutely one in and with all supply.

To help awaken yourself to this state, try to feel yourself in the midst of Infinite abundance much as you might feel yourself in the warmth of the sun while taking a sun bath. After a while, you feel the warmth all through you. At the point of complete oneness, you say, "I am warm." The same situation will prevail when, as, and if, you make your complete oneness with supply as it is.

Train yourself to feel saturated with the Wealth of the Universe. Revel in the sense of infinite wealth that flows toward you, surrounds you, fills you. Let nothing, even poverty itself, dim your realization that: "All the fullness of life, of wealth, of exhaustless abundance is always, everywhere, abundantly manifest. Supply is the self-existent reality of Omnipresence. Abundance is here. It is manifest. All that the God hath is mine now. I simply return to God's house, the state of absolute being where God dwells: am that I am, and beside me there is no other. Therefore, God is all, and is always completely and perfectly and richly manifest."

MEDITATION

"Behold, our God is One, the sum of all things visible and invisible. God is the Wisdom, the Power, and Substance of all things. Therefore, God is the Wealth of Heaven and Earth. The Earth is the Lord's and the fullness thereof, the earth and they that dwell therein—the cattle on a thousand hills—the silver and gold. I live and move and have my being in God, therefore, I move and live and have my being in exhaustless Wealth. God is my Source. It is God that hath made me; I am One with God and the Wealth of God. The very essence and manifestation of Infinite Wealth is in me and through me and around me. Wealth fills me and flows through me. Wealth fills my home, my environment, my affairs, my business, and my world.

"I live perpetually in Wealth, for Wealth is everywhere. All that I can use is always at my command, for it is in me and I am in it.

"Wealth is Infinite and abundantly manifest, for God is Wealth. I am created by Wealth, fashioned of Wealth, live in Wealth, and am of the very substance of Wealth."

Do not let money or the lack of money dull your vision of reality. Do not allow appearances to lull you back into the earth sleep. Awake! Abundance is here now! Live in it until you see its rich manifestation all around you.

The Law of Increase

And all the tithe of the land, whether of the land, whether of the seed of the land, or of the fruit of the tree, is the Lord's: it is holy unto the Lord.

LEVITICUS 27:30

To understand the law of Increase, you first need to understand the importance of tithing. Any practice that endures for centuries must have more than casual importance in human affairs. The further fact that many of the world's greatest credit their success to the practice of tithing also impresses us with its importance.

What is a tithe?

Originally, a tithe was a percentage of flocks, herds, or produce. Incidentally, this percentage given to the Lord was the best of the lot or crop. After the advent of money as a medium of exchange, at least one-tenth of all money received by the individual was turned into religious channels.

It should be remembered that a tithe is neither gift, reward, charity, nor payment for services. It is one-tenth, or more, of your income left with the Source of all things as belonging within and to that Source. It is left that you may not sever your contact with the Source, as did the prodigal son.

The farmer follows the plan of tithing perfectly and scientifically as far as his crops are concerned. Approximately one-tenth of the best seed he raises is kept for replanting. This is returned to the soil to perpetuate the process of growth; that there may be something to perpetuate the Law of Nature. The seed sown is not a gift, nor is it charity, or compensation. It belongs to the soil as an inseparable part of the process of Nature. All increase is contingent upon this procedure. Not only is the best seed saved and used for this purpose, but the ground is prepared and supported in the best possible manner. You see, the farmer protects, preserves, and supports the field from which he directly receives his service.

What is the actual purpose and law of tithing?

The answer is found in Malachi 3:10:

"Bring ye all the tithes into the storehouse, that there may be meat in mine house, and prove me now herewith, saith the Lord of Hosts, if I will not open the windows of Heaven, and pour you out a blessing, that there shall not be room enough to receive it."

THE PURPOSE

It is evident from the above that the first motive of tithing is the support of that Individual or Organization engaged in Spiritual activity, where the knowledge and power of God is promoted. It is definitely for the support of Spiritual Ministries that extend and expand the work of the Creator.

THE LAW

The law of tithing is the law of sowing and reaping. Where there is a definite contact preserved between cause and effect, the effect is supported and perpetuated. If a break in the process occurs, the effect must diminish accordingly. When the prodigal son separated his inheritance from the father, it soon dissipated itself. The law is to perpetuate and amplify whatever it is allowed to act upon. Tithing preserves this contact. It keeps your affairs in contact with creative power. The fruits of the law are contingent upon observance of the law.

To whom is the tithe paid?

In Old Testament times, the tithe went to the support of the Levites (meaning those who adhere) as adherents of the Spiritual Law. They in turn passed on one-tenth of their supply to the support of the priest. In this way, the structure for perpetuating Spiritual ideals was well supported.

One would naturally tithe at that point when direct contact is made with a Spiritual work, be it a structure or function. This is not necessarily the largest Spiritual Organization but that particular Individual or Organization or immediate source from which you are receiving your direct Spiritual help or inspiration. These are all stations in the great order of Spiritual upbuilding. To serve the least of these is to serve the whole. Only through these Spiritual movements have the greatest ideals been preserved, and they are worthy of the greatest cooperation.

Great Spiritual Organizations are built up by great cooperative efforts. A Spiritual Ministry in your locality can be no stronger than the support of its followers will permit. Both Spiritual worker and student of Spiritual things should realize the importance of strong, well-supported points of Spiritual service in a community.

But some say, should not Spiritual work and workers demonstrate their own supply direct? The answer is "yes," but God speaks and acts through you as a channel. You look to the Individual or Organization as a channel through which you receive Spiritual help. In turn, it is perfectly within the province of Spiritual practice that you should be the channel through which God supplies the Minister or the Ministry. "It is a poor rule that does not work both ways."

To safeguard your own best interests, you should make your chosen channel of Spiritual refreshment as strong as possible. You should strive in thought, word, and deed to perfect that channel through which you receive. Or, you should strengthen the channel in your community, for the community's sake, if you have no sense of need for yourself. At the same time, you also provide for those less fortunate than yourself. To make it possible for those around you to receive Spiritual help, you help to lift the standard of your own community and therefore, improve your own environment. This reacts to your greater blessing and advancement.

A starved Spiritual Ministry cannot give to you or your community the best Spiritual support. See that there is "meat in mine house" and the "house" will be in the best possible position to serve you or those about you when any need arises.

How is tithing practiced and what are the results?

THE PRACTICE

To tithe in the true sense, you first set aside one-tenth or more of your whole income. Gifts, charities, obligations, upkeep of relatives, etc., are a matter entirely outside the question of tithing, just as a farmer may give or sell his grain but not the seed reserved for planting his own fields.

The one-tenth set aside as a tithe is never considered your own. It is that portion of income that belongs to the Law, or Source. The first act of the farmer is to select the best seed from the whole crop. The tithe is one-tenth of your entire income first set aside as a "seed" used to maintain contact between the Law and your income.

This tithe is turned back into the Law as soon and as directly as possible. But return your tithe to the storehouse joyously as you would plant a garden. Do not feel you are giving but merely returning to God that which belongs to the Source of all that you are and have. Remember, it is for the purpose of maintaining an unbroken and ever-enlarging contact with the Law of Life, that the action of the Law may be perpetuated in your affairs and the world.

THE RESULTS

When you have tithed directly into the field from which you receive your immediate Spiritual support, you have placed yourself in the most direct position with the law to be assured of the most direct, abundant, and personal blessings. Then the blessings that "maketh rich and addeth no sorrow thereto" are to be expected as your sure reward. Only through preserving your contact with the Law of Life are these blessings to be derived. Ten-, twenty-, fifty- or even a hundred-fold increase is not too much to expect from prompt and complete conformity to the Spirit of the Law.

We do know that through some disobedience to Divine Law, we have received more trouble than we could contain. Why should not a conformity to the Law bring a fulfillment of the promise that our "blessings shall be more than we can contain?" "Prove me now herewith. saith the Lord."

However, the greatest reward is an inner sense that we are in harmony with our own fundamental nature. Inner peace surpasses any outer attainment or material reward. The sense that we are right brings the greatest peace and satisfaction that life affords. Such inner states must have their outer manifestation, for "he that hath the Spirit hath the sign also."

Should those engaged in Spiritual Ministry tithe? Spiritual Teachers and Organizations will also find the practice equally applicable. The Spirit must be the guide as to where the tithe is placed. The order of motives holds good here as elsewhere, however. The Law operates definitely whether given to an Individual engaged in Spiritual ministry or when given to a large well-organized Ministry. Being guided of the Spirit seems the important point. But it is self-evident that a tithe is functioning in its intended sphere only when given to advance a strictly Spiritual activity.

MEDITATION

"Of the increase which life gives to me, I always return one-tenth to my Source. This tenth is in my hand only for the moment as its steward. Returning it immediately to its Source, I keep an unbroken circuit of creative power flowing through me, my business, and my finances.

"The Law of Increase is inevitable and because all things in my life are kept in the stream of life itself, I can logically expect a bountiful increase constantly. There is nothing inanimate, for one Spirit pervades all things. Therefore, my business and finances are always kept vitally animate by this purposefully maintained contact through my tithe.

"The Spirit of God created all things. To support the activity of God as the nearest point where I receive my immediate help, I am promoting the activity of the whole. I thereby preserve the channel of my own good and prepare a fountain of Divine blessing to those about me."

Be thou not afraid when one is made rich,
when the glory of his house is increased;
For when he dieth he shall carry nothing away:
his glory shall not descend after him.

PSALMS 49:16–17